Fruit for Celebrating the Offering

Invitations to Inspire Generosity

By

Melvin Amerson and
James Amerson

Foreword by

Dr. Lovett H. Weems, Jr.

ISBN: 1466457945
ISBN-13: 9781466457942

In our lives we have persons who leave us better because of their inspiration and encouragement. We dedicate this book in loving memory of Mrs. Helen Cox Carline (1919-2011) and Mrs. Jennie L. Carroll (1920-2011)

Statements of Support

"I've found these devotions challenging and thought provoking. Melvin and James use down-to-earth examples to illustrate applications of Scripture verses and stories. Be prepared to be confronted as well as comforted."

– Dr. Ed Kruse, Director for Stewardship,
Evangelical Lutheran Church in America

"These meditations by Melvin and James Amerson will be a helpful companion to persons who invite congregations to worship with the offering week after week. The selections are not written with trendy techniques in mind but are thoughtful, fresh, direct, and motivational to help worshippers grow in the grace of giving with gratitude and spiritual reflection."

– Dr. Leo S. Thorne,
Associate General Secretary,
American Baptist Churches USA

"No more excuses for not moving from vague traditional language to understandable and meaningful offering invitations. In Fruit for Celebrating the Offering, the Amerson brothers have offered meaningful suggestions on how to invite financial support for God's missions in and through the local church."

– Tom Gossen, Executive Director,
The Episcopal Network for Stewardship (TENS)

"The Amerson brothers use fresh, contemporary language in these lively, contextual offering meditations. Their meditations can be used as offering invitations, one of the easiest of stewardship strategies to introduce in a congregation. This book will help liturgists make the offering dynamic and meaningful, inviting people to connect their lives with God's mission through their financial gifts."

– Dr. Barbara Fullerton,
Stewardship Development Program Minister,
United Church of Canada

Foreword

By Dr. Lovett H. Weems, Jr.

When churches face challenging economic times, there is often a debate about the best way to increase funds. Some will put the emphasis on methods and will advocate using the most effective tools available to solicit funds from members. Others will put their emphasis on motivations and will advocate a return to basic spiritual principles from which giving flows.

Those who have studied Christian financial stewardship know that neither approach, to the exclusion of the other, will help move a congregation to where it needs to be. When there is uncertainty and anxiety, no discussion of methods will make sense without biblical and spiritual foundations. It is out of the assurance that God's care is from everlasting, and God has promised never to leave us abandoned, that we can put our money in its rightful perspective in God's universe. But even with an emphasis on motivation, people will need encouragement as well as information about various ways to give. While never confusing the earthen vessels with the treasure, leaders will find it important to draw wisdom from many sources to craft fruitful means form any particular season.

Melvin and James Amerson have provided a resource for church leaders that helps to bring together the spiritual and practical. One lesson is that people need to be reminded of the importance of giving. The authors take something that many church members see as merely utilitarian ("we have to pay the bills") and remind people of the great spiritual significance of the act of offering in worship. The meditations they have prepared for pastors and lay leaders give important spiritual reminders to bring to the congregation – calling all of us to offer to God our gifts as one part of our offering of all we have and are.

– Dr. Lovett H. Weems, Jr.
Distinguished Professor of Church Leadership and
Director of the Lewis Center for Church Leadership
Wesley Theological Seminary
Washington, DC

Fruit for Celebrating the Offering

Invitations to Inspire Generosity

By

**Melvin Amerson and
James Amerson**

Introduction

The offertory during worship is often viewed as the time during the service where the pastor "asks or pleas" for help with the church's bills. Sadly, this is how many congregations perceive the offering. The offering is far more than merely asking for money to pay the pastor's salary, providing support for the church's ministries or keeping the lights on. When we give an offering during worship, we are indeed worshipping God through our giving. Giving is an awesome act of worship.

In many cases the offering does not receive much in the way of spiritual importance. Pastors and worship leaders simply go through the motion. The ushers are called forward to receive the offering plate from either the pastor or worship leader; a prayer is briefly offered; the ushers are sent out; and shortly thereafter the plates are returned and the congregation joins in by singing the Doxology. The act of honoring God is over in a mere sigh. A few intentional biblically-based words of encouragement, hope, faith and trust will shed a new light on the offering. Moreover, these words will give believers insightful ways to see their lives as Christian stewards and believers in the body of Christ.

Fruit for Celebrating the Offering provides offering invitations to be shared weekly before the offering to help set the tone for worship through giving, and to develop a spirit and culture of generosity within a congregation of believers. Further, these invitations will provide an insightful and spiritually thought provoking way to look at our giving. Both clergy and laity may use these invitations week after week to share with members how their gifts honor God, and provide resources for ministry for both their local church community and also those with a greater global mission.

It is our prayer that this book of offering invitations will help with the transformation of hearts, such that they will be filled with the spirit of generosity and in turn lead to ample resources for building up the Kingdom of God.

Notes or Reflections

3/17/19

Parents often give increases in their children's allowance as they mature. Typically, with the increase there is an increase in responsibility. God does the same with adults. He increases our earnings and provision, so in turn, we are able to give more to disciple-building ministries. It is said in Luke 12:48. "To whom much is given, even much more will be required." Let us worship the Lord in our giving.

Notes or Reflections

3/24/19

I heard a pastor once say, "You can't pay God back, but you can pay God forward." Consider giving as the Lord has blessed you. Joshua 24:15 says, "…for me and my household, we will serve the Lord." Part of serving the Lord is presenting his tithes and our offerings unto him. Let us present our tithes and offerings from this day forward.

Notes or Reflections

Sunday March 31

"Give and it will be given to you pressed down, shaken together, running over, will be put into your lap, for the measure you give will be the measure you get back." Luke 6:38. This verse of scripture sounds like an investment plan. God's tithes and offerings are much like a mutual fund. When we give collectively as a body of believers, that is what will occur in our congregation. The overflow of resources can be used to further transform lives and build the Kingdom of God. Let us present our tithes and offerings into God's mutual fund.

Notes or Reflections

There was a time when sports agents would earn a fee of 10% of an athlete's contract just for negotiating the contract. The agent would receive the entire amount off the top regardless of what took place after the signing of that contract. For some reason people resist giving a tithe or 10% to God, who negotiates every turn and facet of our lives. Let us present our tithes in gratitude for what the Lord continuously does for us.

Notes or Reflections

4/7/19

"For where your treasure is, there your heart be also." Matthew 6:21. This verse is so true when we examine our checkbook or credit card statement. God calls us to be generous as he has been generous to us. The things we treasure we tend to eagerly support. How does your support of the Lord's work measure with the other things you treasure? Let us give as God has generously given to us.

Notes or Reflections

"The one who sows sparingly will also reap sparingly, and the one who sows abundantly will also reap abundantly." II Corinthians 9:6. After reading that verse of scripture, one would begin to think about seeds and how they come in a variety of sizes and shapes. I would also imagine not all seeds would be perfect; some would be cracked, rotten, broken or underdeveloped. However, there will be plenty of good seeds with the potential to produce a great plant and in turn an abundant harvest. Giving is about the spirit in which we sow seeds in God's work. God wants our gifts to grow and develop into life-transforming ministries. Let us sow healthy producing seeds for the building of God's Kingdom.

Notes or Reflections

There are two types of quarterbacks and givers. One stays in the pocket, and that is what happens with many givers when it is time to give to the Lord's work. The other, a scrambler, is one who does whatever is necessary to advance the cause. Are you going to be a stay in the pocket giver or scrambler? Let us scramble into our pockets to give a generous offering.

Notes or Reflections

The Lord's assurance covers us in every facet of our lives. Jesus' death and resurrection paid for all of those assurances in full, which comes in the form of protection, provisions, and other blessings. The tithes and offerings we bring week after week demonstrate our gratitude for the Lord's assurances. Let us give to assure God's blessings to others near and far.

Notes or Reflections

The psalmist tells us in Psalm 24:1. "The earth is the Lord's and all that is in it." That verse reminds me of a song that is still being sung by children today, "He's got the Whole World in His Hands." If God has us in his hands, and everything belongs to him, may we give praise and honor to the Lord with a generous offering in thanks for his awesome generosity and caring hands.

Notes or Reflections

In the Parable of the Sower, the Sower sowed seeds in a variety of soil, which had mixed results. Seeds sown into God's church that transforms lives and communities are the equivalent of sowing seeds into good soil. Let us sow seeds into God's fertile ministries.

Notes or Reflections

4-14-19

You may not believe it, but you are blessed materially. In our country we have more than the majority of people in the world. With that particular fact comes responsibility; "To whom much has been given, much will be required and from the one to whom much has been entrusted, even more will be demanded." (Luke 12:48) Giving to the Lord's work helps us grow spiritually, and bless others who are in need. Let us give as the blessed people that we are.

Notes or Reflections

Apostle Paul said in (I Corinthians 4:2) "Moreover, it is required of stewards to be found trustworthy." As believers we are stewards or managers of all the resources God has entrusted to us. God calls us to manage and use his resources in a way that glorifies him. We honor God in how we earn, save, and give. Let us give as trustworthy stewards for the Lord's Kingdom building works.

Notes or Reflections

Most gifts we are able to describe and give accurate descriptions of. Further, we can articulate the benefits and the uses of the gift. (II Corinthians 9:15) says, "Thanks be to God for his indescribable gift!" God's indescribable gift is his grace, which he generously showers upon us all. Our giving in worship is to honor the Lord for his indescribable gift. Let us give in response to God's gift of grace and generosity.

Notes or Reflections

Have you thought about why (Proverbs 3:9) says "Honor the Lord with your substance and with the first fruits of all your produce"? For a moment think about the longevity of fresh fruit or vegetables. After a week the fresh produce has to be thrown away because it is no longer edible or has value. That is why we are to honor the Lord with our first fruits. Let us honor the Lord with our first and best gifts.

Notes or Reflections

Jacob, in the twenty-eighth chapter of Genesis, had a dream of a ladder extending up to heaven with angels of God ascending and descending. After his dream, he said; "If God will be with me and provide for me, I will call this place Bethel, the House of God." Then he made a vow to give a tenth of all that God had given him. Are we waiting to have the same dream as Jacob before we make a vow to return a tenth to God? Let us give now as a response to how God has blessed us.

Notes or Reflections

King David told his people in (I Chronicles 29:14) "But who am I, and what are my people, that we should be able to make this freewill offering? For all things come from you, and of your own have we given you." The latter portion of that verse is the biblical basis for a familiar doxology. We acknowledge our blessings from God, but are we responding to God's abundant generosity with generous gifts as a sign of gratitude? Let us present a gift to God that is pleasing and acceptable in his sight.

Notes or Reflections

"All things come from thee O' Lord, and of thine own have we given thee." (I Chronicles 29:14) Sunday after Sunday, we sing this doxology after receiving the offering. Many of us sing this doxology as a weekly ritual, without really understanding its true meaning. This verse acknowledges that everything belongs to God, and we give a small portion back to the Lord to show our thanks, praise and gratitude. Let us give as good stewards, and sing the doxology; "All things come from thee oh Lord, and of thine own have we given thee." Let us sing it, like we believe it!

Notes or Reflections

God asks us to be faithful stewards. When we are faithful to what God calls us to do and be, then we will find ourselves in a position to receive his blessings. Jesus said, "Whoever is faithful in very little is faithful also in much." (Luke 16:10) Let us be faithful in the presentation of our tithes and offerings.

Notes or Reflections

The book of Acts tells us about the early church and how committed the believers were to sharing with one another so no one had a need. They sold all their possessions to make sure needs were satisfied. God does not require us to sell all of our possessions, but he does expect us to provide for those who are less fortunate. Let us give so we will have resources for God's church and its life sustaining and transforming ministries.

Notes or Reflections

Apostle Paul in (II Corinthians 8:12) said, "For if the eagerness is there, the gift is acceptable according to what one has, not according to what one does not have." As we prepare to worship the Lord through giving, display your eagerness in response to how the Lord has blessed you. Let us eagerly present our tithes and offering so we are able to support God's Kingdom building works.

Notes or Reflections

In elementary school I recall a saying "April showers bring May flowers." It is the same with us. God plants seeds inside each of us, showers us with grace, which blossoms into disciples and generous givers. Ministries of the church and lives will blossom when we support them. Let us give generously to the ministries that God has planted here.

Notes or Reflections

In the parable of the talents Jesus taught; we are to invest and not hoard what we have been entrusted with in building up the Kingdom. If we use what God has invested in us, he will multiply it into life transforming blessings. As stewards, God wants us to invest our talents and financial resources for his disciple making enterprise. Let us give faithfully to honor God for the many blessings that he showers upon us.

Notes or Reflections

The widow in the parable of the "Widow's Mite" gave all that she had as an offering. Some of us contend we cannot give, others say, "I might give, if…" The latter "MIGHT" indicates the gift is based on a set of conditions like, "if I get this" or "when this happens." God could tell us, "I might supply all your needs." For God there is no "might," he truly does provide abundantly. Let us give like the widow who gave her best and gave out of her unconditional love.

Notes or Reflections

Apostle Paul said, "They voluntarily gave according to their means and even beyond their means." (II Corinthians 8:3) The poor Macedonian Church members did not limit their generosity due to their limited resources, but rejoiced in the opportunity to support the ministry. Have you ever considered giving like the members of the Macedonian Church who gave beyond their means? Let us consider an offering beyond our normal gifts to further ministries near and far.

Notes or Reflections

Author, Lynn Miller, described generosity as love in action. The early church depicted in Acts 2 shows believers who sold their possessions so others could have plenty. Their generosity exemplifies God's love. As we prepare for the offering, remember, "Love your neighbor as you love yourself." Let us give our gifts so we may glorify God and bless our neighbors.

Notes or Reflections

Apostle Paul said they voluntarily gave according to their means, and even beyond their means. The poor Macedonia Church members did not limit their generosity because of their limited resources, but rejoiced in the opportunity to support another ministry. Have you considered giving beyond your current level of comfort to support life-changing ministries? Let us consider a gift beyond our regular giving to help expand God's Kingdom.

Notes or Reflections

Many of you may not believe it, but God wants us to be prosperous and rich. We all have different ideas or definitions for "rich." Apostle Paul in (I Timothy 6:18) "They are to do good, to be rich in good works, generous, and ready to share." Let us be rich, generous and ready to share in our offerings that will enable us to make a difference in God's Kingdom.

Notes or Reflections

Our U.S. currency has a quote imprinted on every coin and bill which says, "In God We Trust." Some of us trust God only when our pockets or bank accounts are full. Our real trust in God lies within our faith. It is written in (Hebrews 11:1) "Now faith is the evidence of things hopeful, substance of things not seen." Giving is a measure of our trust and faith in God. Let us give in a manner, which demonstrates our trust and faith in God that he will supply all of our needs in Christ Jesus.

Notes or Reflections

"Money is the root of all evil," is an often misstated verse in the Bible. The accurate quote of that particular verse is "The love of money is the root of all evil." God calls us to give freely as he has given to us so that money will not possess us and become a barrier to our relationship with him. Let us show our love for the Lord as we present our tithes and offerings.

Notes or Reflections

The television game show "Let's Make A Deal" was based on contestants betting or trading in hopes of winning the grand prize. There was always the risk of losing everything. God made a covenant with us to supply all of our needs, and made us his stewards. Let us honor God with our first fruits for his mighty and endless faithfulness.

Notes or Reflections

In the parable of the "Rich Fool or Farmer" he spent his life accumulating more and more things. Has "stuff" become your priority? God asked the farmer, "Who will ultimately inherit your earthly goods?" "The truth is, the earth is the Lord's and all that is in it." (Psalm 24:1) God only requires us to give back a small portion of our income in the form of our tithes and offerings. Let us give generously so that we may honor God and bless others.

Notes or Reflections

In (Matthew 6:24) Jesus said, "No one can serve two masters; one will either hate the one and love the other, or be devoted to the one and despise the other. You cannot serve God and wealth." The presentation of our tithes and offering is God's way of helping us overcome our personal struggle with materialism and consumerism while worshipping him. Let us give generously to our master, the God all mighty.

Notes or Reflections

Apostle Paul said in (I Corinthians 16:2) "On the first day of every week each of you is to put aside and save whatever extra you earn, so that collections need not be taken when I come." In this verse he informs believers their offerings are more than an occasional gift; it is worship. Today, we also believe our regular offering is a part of worshipping God. As God has prospered you, may you also remember your worship through giving.

Notes or Reflections

There are several passages in the Bible where seeds are used in allegories to show God's promise when believers sow seeds in faith. Financial gifts the church receives are seeds filled with the potential of providing a harvest of life transforming ministries. Let us honor the Lord with fertile seeds to be planted into the Lord's life-changing mission field.

Notes or Reflections

In (Matthew 22:37-38) Jesus tells us of the two greatest commandments. "Love the Lord, your God with all your heart and with all your soul" and "Love your neighbor as yourself." When we combine these two commandments we should feel compelled to show our love with our offerings. Our offering honors the Lord and allows us to show compassion for our neighbors who are in need. Let us give so that we may display our love for God and neighbors near and far.

Notes or Reflections

Healthy fruit trees grow, mature, and produce fruit. The same is true with Christians who grow and mature. They grow in faith and bear fruit. Our giving grows as we mature in our faith and our gifts bear fruit in the form of fruitful ministry. Let our gifts bear fruit in life transforming ministries.

Notes or Reflections

On U.S. paper currency the word "note" is inscribed. Sheet music also contains "notes." Musical notes are made up of different sound values, which are held for different lengths of time. Harmonious music is created in hymns and anthems through a series of sound values of eighth notes, quarter notes, half notes and whole notes. As we prepare for worship through giving, let us increase the value of our notes so our offering will create harmonious resources for ministry.

Notes or Reflections

Apostle Paul tells us in (Philippians 2:4-5) "Let each of you look not to your own interests, but to the interests of others. Let the same mind be in you that was in Christ Jesus." Our gifts are an extension of ourselves to others. Let us give for the benefit of others as Christ gave of himself.

Notes or Reflections

(Luke 17:11-19) tells the story of Jesus healing the lepers. One of the lepers happened to come back to show his gratitude. The weekly offering is an opportunity to come back to show our gratitude for what God has done in our lives. As we prepare for the offering let us show our gratitude with the presentation of our tithes and offerings.

Notes or Reflections

Apostle Paul spoke to his friends in (Galatians 6:2) and told them. "Bear one another's burden and in this way you will fulfill the law of Christ." As believers, we are called to bear one another's burdens and inequalities among those who are in need. Let us give generously to glorify the Lord in our missional work.

Notes or Reflections

"The earth is the Lord's and all that is in it." Psalm 24:1. If all that we have belongs to God, then the presentation of our tithes and offerings are a mere partial return. Let us prayerfully consider returning a generous portion unto the Lord of ministry.

Notes or Reflections

The Bible tells us in (Galatians 6:10) "Whenever we have an opportunity, let us work for the good of all..." Our tithes and offerings provide resources and opportunities to be a blessing to others. Here is the opportunity for us to minister for the good of all in God's Kingdom. Let us seize the opportunity to give generously to God's great works.

Notes or Reflections

Some of us are picky eaters when it comes to fruit. Have you ever chosen some fruits over others? The least popular fruit listed in the "Fruits of the Spirit" in (Galatians) is probably the spiritual fruit of generosity. It is not very popular in our culture because it calls us to give. Let us embrace the spirit of generosity to shower and bless others who are in need. Today, allow your spiritual fruit of generosity to flourish and honor God.

Notes or Reflections

Jesus said in (John 8:12) "I am the light of the world. Whoever follows me will never walk in darkness, but will have the light of life." It is through our giving we are able to provide much needed resources for life changing ministries to persons around the world so they may discover the light of others. Let us give so others will know Jesus is the light of the world.

Notes or Reflections

Jesus was prompted to share the parable of the "Good Samaritan" when a lawyer asked; "And who is my neighbor?" As the story goes, others passed the injured man, but the Samaritan stopped and rendered aid and went into his own pocket to assist the stranger. When we give, it should not matter who our neighbor is or whether we can identify with them in their situation. Our offering is a sign of our unconditional love for our neighbors near and far. Remember, we are to love our neighbors as we love ourselves. Let us give so we can share with our neighbors.

Notes or Reflections

The Dead Sea is a salty body of water that does not possess any living organism. The sediments that flow into the Dead Sea have no way of being filtered or released. The waters flowing from running streams and rivers are full of living organisms. As believers, we have a choice of being like a life giving river or a receptor like the Dead Sea. The offering we give during worship is life altering. Let us give so we can make a difference in the lives of others.

Notes or Reflections

(II Corinthians 8:15) reads, "The one who had much did not have too much, and the one who had little did not have too little." This passage encourages us to give generously regardless of whether we are blessed with much or little. Our giving can produce the needed resources to ensure vital ministries that touch the lives of those who are in need. Let us give generously in response to God's grace and generosity.

Notes or Reflections

"Thanks be to God for his indescribable gifts," is a powerful acknowledgement of the sovereignty of God by Apostle Paul. God's generosity is an outflow of his gift of grace. Something described as indescribable is often an action or object that is so awesome that few words can adequately describe or explain it. This is our opportunity to respond generously to God's indescribable gift of grace. Freely give, freely receive.

Notes or Reflections

Believe it or not, in (Exodus 36:1-7) Moses once had to restrain his people from bringing their offerings for the building of their sanctuary because they had brought more than enough for the work at hand. In their case, their gifts were for a new sanctuary, but our gifts are for life changing ministries, which are ongoing. God is calling us to give more so we can do more for the Kingdom. Let us give generously and faithfully to build God's ongoing Kingdom.

Notes or Reflections

(I John 3:17-18) provides a special question and answer about the responsibilities of believers. "How does God's love abide in anyone who has the world's goods and sees a brother or sister in need, yet refuses to help?" Little children let us love, not in word or speech, but in truth and action. That is our question and answer to our responsibility to others. The presentation of our tithes and offerings is a tangible way to assist those who are in need. Let us give generously to help those who need a hand.

Notes or Reflections

Moses in (Deuteronomy 15:7) said, "Do not be hard-hearted or tight-fisted toward your needy neighbor." Bearing a hard heart or a closed hand prevents blessings from flowing out to others in need. When we give generously we are able to be a blessing to others while maintaining a caring heart and open hand. Let us present our gifts unto the Lord for the good of others.

Notes or Reflections

Apostle Paul said, "For if the eagerness is there, the gift is acceptable to what one has, not according to what one does not have." God looks more towards the eagerness and cheerfulness in our hearts than the amount we give. When we give, we honor God, give thanks and share with others. With great eagerness let us prepare for the presentation of our tithes and offerings unto the Lord.

Notes or Reflections

"If you have faith the size of a mustard seed... and nothing will be impossible for you." (Matthew 17:20) The mustard seed is a very tiny seed, but it has the potential to grow into an enormous plant. All of our gifts are small compared to what God has provided for us. However, when our gifts are combined together and blessed with the faith and trust in the Lord, they will mushroom into abundant resources for growing ministries. Let us remember our giving is a matter of faith and trust.

Notes or Reflections

"The one who had much did not have too much and the one who had little did not have too little." (II Corinthians 8:15) We have all been blessed with varying resources, some with more than others. Our gifts provide resources for life sustaining ministries, and narrows the gap between the *haves*, and the *have not's* both in our local community and around the world. Let us give generously so all may have some.

Notes or Reflections

(Proverbs 19:17) tells us, "Whoever is kind to the poor lends to the Lord, and will be repaid in full." Believers give out of the kindness of their hearts to glorify the Lord. Our gifts honor God and bless those who are in need. When we give out of the kindness of our hearts, God repays and blesses us in a multitude of ways. Allow your spirit of generosity to overflow from your heart for the benefit and blessings of others.

Notes or Reflections

"Those who are generous are blessed for they share their bread with the poor." (Proverbs 22:9) Generosity flows from one to another. When we are generous with others, their personal names and location of residence is of little importance, for we know our generosity is an extension of God's love for humanity. Blessings are received when we share God's gifts, which he has generously bestowed upon us. Let us give so others will have.

Notes or Reflections

"Let everything that has breath praise ye the Lord." That alone is something to get excited about. God goes way beyond giving us breath. He gives us life, food, shelter, family and friends, just to mention a few. Out of gratitude we praise the Lord. "Praise God from whom all blessings flow." Let us praise him with a generous offering for giving us an abundant life.

Notes or Reflections

In (I Chronicles 29) King David rejoiced along with the men and women who gave with a single mind for the purpose of building the temple. At the time of the offering, we ought to be of one mind rejoicing and responding to God's grace and generosity. Our giving serves as a witness to our oneness as laborers in God's vineyard. Let us be of one mind as we celebrate the offering.

Notes or Reflections

World Communion Sunday

World Communion Sunday is a day of worship where Christians from all denominations around the world will celebrate and affirm Holy Communion as Christ's offering to us. Christ gave his "all" for the good of humankind; this means that we are all connected as believers. This special offering reinforces our relationship to Christ and others who share in Holy Communion. Let us give generously for the good of mission and ministry here and around the world.

Notes or Reflections

Thanksgiving

Many associate Thanksgiving with turkey, parades, and football. In reality those things actually have little to do with the spirit of Thanksgiving. It is okay to recognize those things that are often associated with Thanksgiving, if they do not cloud or overshadow the true meaning and purpose. Thanksgiving is about giving thanks for God's generosity. Our response to God's generosity should be displayed with a tangible gift as a sign of our love and gratitude for all God has done for us. Let us share a special gift of thanks as a sign of love for God and others.

Notes or Reflections

Christmas

This is the time of the year where individuals give gifts, receive gifts or take time off from work for the Christmas holidays. In the midst of the classic seasonal Christmas movies and cartoons, not to mention commercial Christmas advertisements, we often overlook the true meaning of the season. We all know the true meaning of Christmas centers on the birth of Jesus the Christ, a child also known as the Prince of Peace. Let us honor Jesus with a gift of generosity worthy of a Savior.

52551491R00076

Made in the USA
Columbia, SC
04 March 2019